D1221035

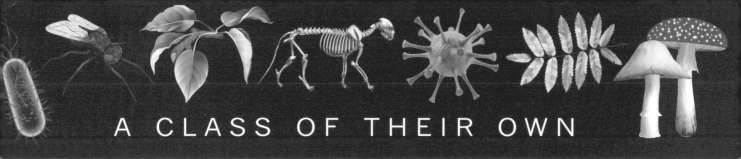

A CLASS OF THEIR OWN

Archaea

Salt-lovers, Methane-makers,
Thermophiles, and Other Archaeans

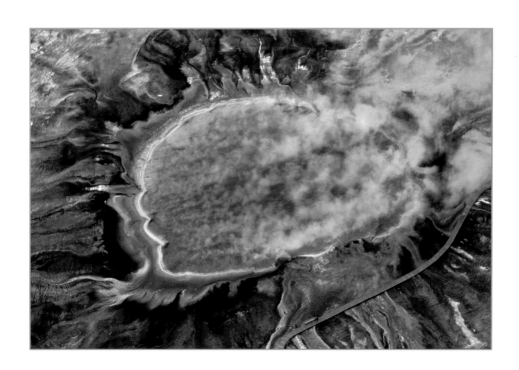

By
David M. Barker

Crabtree Publishing Company
www.crabtreebooks.com

Crabtree Publishing Company

www.crabtreebooks.com

Author: David M. Barker
Series consultant: Sally Morgan, MA, MSc, MIBiol
Project director: Ruth Owen
Designer: Alix Wood
Editors: Mark Sachner, Adrianna Morganelli
Proofreader: Crystal Sikkens
Project manager: Kathy Middleton
Production coordinator: Katherine Berti
Prepress technician: Katherine Berti

Developed & Created by **Ruby Tuesday Books Ltd**

Front cover: A colored scanning electron micrograph (SEM) of
Pyrococcus furiosus. This archaean lives in near-boiling
water in undersea hot water vents.

Title page: The Grand Prismatic Spring, a hot spring at
Yellowstone National Park, U.S.

Photographs:
Ecoscene: pages 16, 31
FLPA: pages 4, 8
Bill Gilhooly: page 19 (inset)
Dr. Alison Murray: page 28 (top)
NASA: pages 28 (center left), 28 (center bottom)
Ruby Tuesday Books Ltd: pages 12, 41
Science Photo Library: front cover, pages 6, 7, 9 (left), 10 (top),
    10 (bottom), 11, 13, 18–19 (main), 21 (main), 21 (inset), 24,
    26 (background/main), 30, 32 (main), 36, 37, 42, 43 (bottom)
Shutterstock: pages 9 (right), 15, 23, 28 (background), 29, 32 (top),
    33, 35, 38–39 (main), 39 (inset), 40
Wikipedia: pages 1, 14, 22, 25, 26 (top), 27, 43 (top)

Library and Archives Canada Cataloguing in Publication

Barker, David, 1959-
    Archaea : salt-lovers, methane-makers, thermophiles, and
other archaea / David M. Barker.

(A class of their own)
Includes index.
ISBN 978-0-7787-5373-5 (bound).--ISBN 978-0-7787-5387-2 (pbk.)

    1. Archaebacteria--Classification--Juvenile literature.
2. Archaebacteria--Juvenile literature. I. Title.
II. Series: Class of their own

QR82.A69B37 2010   j579.3'21012   C2009-907486-9

Library of Congress Cataloging-in-Publication Data

Barker, David. (David M.)
 Archaea : salt-lovers, methane-makers, thermophiles, and other archaeans /
by David Barker.
    p. cm. -- (A class of their own)
 Includes index.
 ISBN 978-0-7787-5387-2 (pbk. : alk. paper) -- ISBN 978-0-7787-5373-5
(reinforced library binding : alk. paper)
 1. Archaebacteria--Juvenile literature. I. Title. II. Series.

QR82.A69B37 2010
579.3'21--dc22

2009051393

Crabtree Publishing Company

www.crabtreebooks.com   1-800-387-7650

Printed in the U.S.A./012010/BG20091216

Published in Canada
Crabtree Publishing
616 Welland Ave.
St. Catharines, Ontario
L2M 5V6

Published in the United States
Crabtree Publishing
PMB 59051
350 Fifth Avenue, 59th Floor
New York, New York 10118

Published in the United Kingdom
Crabtree Publishing
Maritime House
Basin Road North, Hove
BN41 1WR

Published in Australia
Crabtree Publishing
386 Mt. Alexander Rd.
Ascot Vale (Melbourne)
VIC 3032

Contents

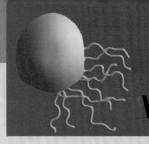
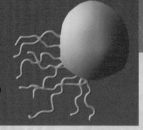

WHAT ARE ARCHAEANS?

The amazing scenery of Yellowstone National Park attracts more than two million visitors each year. They come to see the brightly colored hot springs, the erupting geysers, and the wildlife. The hot springs are a magnet for scientists, too, but for a completely different reason.

A "New" Life-form

It was here in the 1970s that a whole new group of organisms was discovered, living in what was thought to be a completely inhospitable habitat for life. The discovery of this new life-form has revolutionized biology, causing biologists to rethink the way they classified organisms.

CASE STUDY

Kingdom or Domain?

EUKARYA

Protists
Plants
Animals
Fungi

BACTERIA

ARCHAEA

The way life-forms are grouped, or classified, is constantly changing. Traditionally, organisms were classified as either animal or plant. Over the years, many organisms have been grouped *alongside* animals and plants, rather than *within* those two groups. For years, the classification of living things has been based on six *kingdoms* of life—animals, plants, fungi, protists, bacteria, and archaea.

As scientists improve their understanding of the genetic makeup of living things, they can better compare organisms. This understanding has helped scientists figure out even more detailed groupings of living things. In the past, organisms were grouped according to their appearance. Appearances can be misleading, however. Two organisms may look similar, but their genetic makeup can be very different. For example, some yeasts might be taken for bacteria based on the fact that, like bacteria, they consist of a single round cell. Today, yeasts are known to be fungi, not bacteria.

Most scientists now believe that organisms should be classified using an even bigger grouping than kingdom. This level is called the *domain*. These scientists propose that life should be divided into three domains—Eukarya, Bacteria, and Archaea. Within the domain Eukarya are the four kingdoms for animals, plants, fungi, and protists. These kingdoms are more closely related to each other than to the domains for bacteria and archaea.

This is where things stand—for now. As scientists continue to make new discoveries, this system will undoubtedly turn out to be another chapter in the story of life!

Ancient Things

In the late 1970s, the biologist Thomas Brock collected some unusual bacteria living in the hot springs in Yellowstone National Park. The cells were interesting because they could survive in temperatures close to the boiling point of water. These temperatures would kill most life on Earth. Another biologist, Carl Woese, studied a part of the DNA of these cells. He examined a gene that is found in all living things and found something unusual. The units of the DNA were in a sequence that was completely different from bacteria, and different from eukaryotes. Originally life was like a tree that had two branches, prokaryotes and eukaryotes. Dr. Woese now believed that he had found a third branch. He called that third branch *Archaebacteria* (ar-kee-bak-teer-ee-ah), which soon became *Archaea* (ar-kee-ah), a word that means "ancient things."

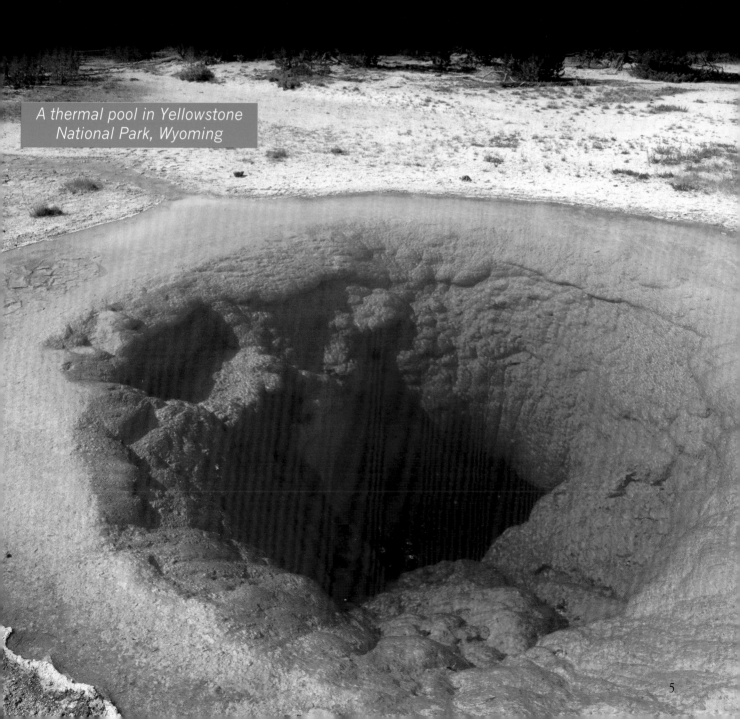

A thermal pool in Yellowstone National Park, Wyoming

Over the last 30 years, many different types of archaeans have been discovered, many living in the most inhospitable places on the planet—in boiling mud, in salty water, in the deepest oceans, in the guts of animals, and even in oil in the ground. These exciting organisms have changed how we understand all life on Earth, and they have even changed how we think about extraterrestrial life.

Kingdom to Species

Scientists have identified about two million species, or types, of organisms, and it is likely that many more millions of species are still to be discovered. With so many species, scientists have always needed to organize them. They first organized them into groups of organisms that looked similar. Now the groups are meant to show how living organisms are related to one another. First, living organisms are divided into three broad groups called domains. The domains are Archaea, Bacteria, and Eukarya. Eukarya includes animals, plants, fungi, and protists. Each domain is divided into kingdoms, which are also large groups. Each kingdom is divided into phyla (singular *phylum*), which are divided into classes, and then orders, families, genera (singular *genus*), and finally species.

Classifying Organisms

Domain

Kingdom

Phylum

Class

Order

Family

Genus

Species

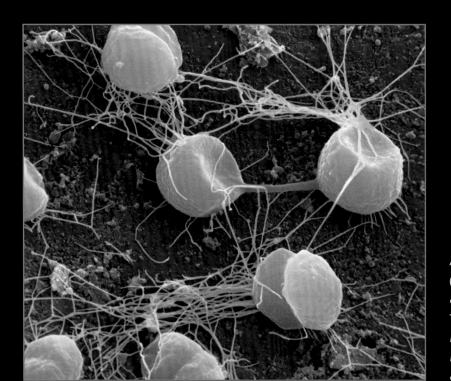

A scanning electron micrograph (SEM) of the hyperthermophile archaean species Pyrococcus furiosus, *which lives in undersea hot vents. It survives near-boiling water, lack of oxygen, and great pressure.*

Naming Organisms

Each species has a unique name that is made up of two words. The first word is the name of the genus to which the organism belongs, and the second word is the name of the species. Because archaeans are new to science and hard to see, they do not have many common names. You won't find a "red-bellied sapsucker" among archaean names. They have the Latin and Greek names that scientists give to all living things. These can be difficult to say and read. This book will show how to pronounce many of the names and sometimes what the Latin and Greek roots mean. When scientists give a name to an archaean, it is usually the Latin or Greek word for something special about that organism, like a code name for the organism.

Classifying the Archaea

The domain Archaea is divided into five phyla. The first phylum is Crenarchaeota (kren-ar-kee-ota), meaning "spring ancient things." The word *spring* means these cells were thought to be most like the original archaeans in the way springs are the origins of streams. This is a very diverse group of archaeans, typical of extremely hot and acidic environments, and many feed on sulfur.

The second phylum is Euryarchaeota (yur-ee-ar-kee-o-tah), meaning "broad ancient things," because these cells were found in many different habitats. This phylum includes two large groups: the halophiles, or salt-lovers, and the methanogens, or methane-makers. There are also some thermophiles that can cope with high temperatures and also a few psychrophiles that live in very cold conditions. Most of the Euryarchaeota are mesophiles, however, living in habitats with a normal range of temperatures.

A "black smoker" vent on the ocean floor deep below the Atlantic Ocean. Here, sulfurous, mineral-rich water heated by Earth's magma—at temperatures of 680°F (360°C)—bubbles up through Earth's crust. This unusual habitat is home to sulfur-loving archaeans.

More recently, three new phyla of archaeans have been described. The first of these is Korarchaeota (kor-ark-ee-o-tah), meaning "young ancient things." Again, scientists wanted to describe these as primitive, or young, archaeans. They have only been found in extremely high-temperature environments, such as hydrothermal vents on the deep seabed.

The fourth phylum is called Nanoarchaeota (nan-o-ar-kee-o-tah), meaning "very small ancient things." There is only one species in this phylum, *Nanoarchaeum equitans*, which was found in a hydrothermal vent in 2002 by Karl Stetter.

The most recently proposed phylum, Thaumarchaeota, is made up of archaeans that were once classified within the phylum Crenarchaeota. These archaeans have an important role to play in natural cycles, such as the nitrogen cycle.

Classification in Archaea is changing often as new species are found and described. Even after more than 30 years since their discovery, there are only several hundred species of archaeans described by scientists. They know there are many more out there to be discovered. Stay tuned for frequent updates.

Microbiologist Dr. Karl Stetter, collecting samples in the Valley of the Geysers, Kronotsky Nature Reserve, Kamchatka, Russia.

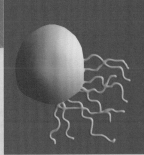
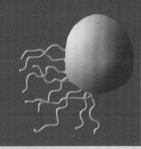

CHAPTER ONE

THE BIOLOGY OF ARCHAEANS

Archaeans are tiny single-celled organisms, most of which are less than one micrometer across. That's one-thousandth of a millimeter in diameter. The largest reach 15 micrometers. Compare that to a human hair, which is about 100 micrometers across.

Electron Microscopes Needed

To see these organisms you have to magnify them a lot. If you looked at them using a light microscope that you would find in a school science lab, you would just see a small dot. To see the details of these cells, we must view them with a very powerful microscope, called an electron microscope. These microscopes magnify the image of the organism many thousands of times.

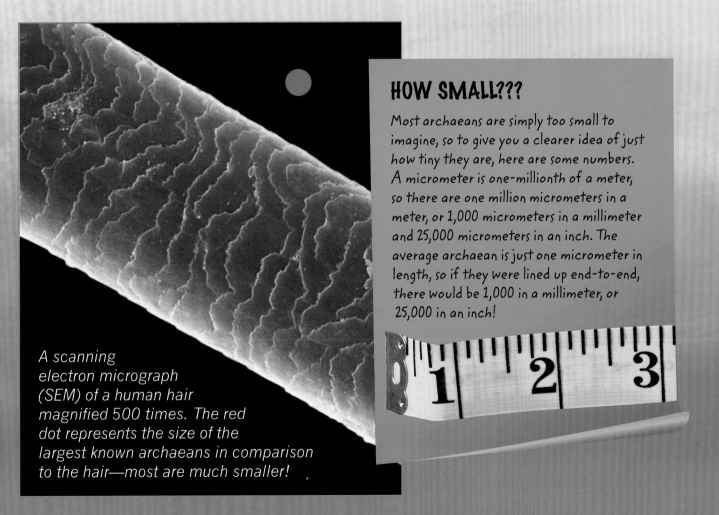

A scanning electron micrograph (SEM) of a human hair magnified 500 times. The red dot represents the size of the largest known archaeans in comparison to the hair—most are much smaller!

HOW SMALL???

Most archaeans are simply too small to imagine, so to give you a clearer idea of just how tiny they are, here are some numbers. A micrometer is one-millionth of a meter, so there are one million micrometers in a meter, or 1,000 micrometers in a millimeter and 25,000 micrometers in an inch. The average archaean is just one micrometer in length, so if they were lined up end-to-end, there would be 1,000 in a millimeter, or 25,000 in an inch!

Inside the Cell

The structure of the archaean cell—and that of the bacterium—is different from that of animals and plants. If you were to look at a cell taken from the lining of your mouth under a powerful microscope, you would see a relatively large cell made up of a jelly-like substance called cytoplasm. It is surrounded by a cell membrane that acts as a barrier. Floating in the cytoplasm are small structures called organelles, the largest of which is the nucleus. The nucleus contains the genetic material—the DNA—and it is surrounded by a membrane. The membrane controls what goes into and out of the nucleus. There are other organelles, too—for example, mitochondria, which are often described as the cell's powerhouses as they release energy for the cell to use. The cells of plants, fungi, and protists have a membrane-bound nucleus, too. Organisms with this cell structure are called eukaryotes.

Bacteria and archaeans are different. They are single-celled organisms called prokaryotes. Their cell structure is much simpler than the eukaryotes. There is a cell membrane surrounding the cytoplasm but there is no nucleus or other membrane-bound organelles. Instead, there is a large loop of DNA lying in the cytoplasm. There are also plasmids, which are very small loops of DNA.

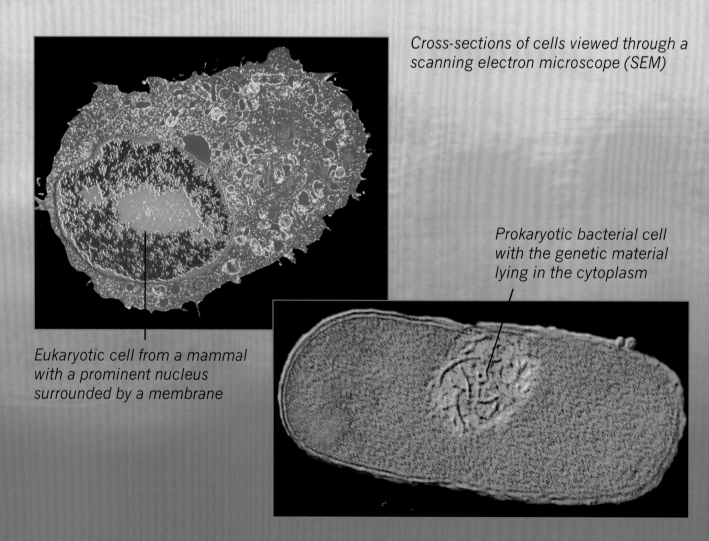

Cross-sections of cells viewed through a scanning electron microscope (SEM)

Prokaryotic bacterial cell with the genetic material lying in the cytoplasm

Eukaryotic cell from a mammal with a prominent nucleus surrounded by a membrane

As well as a membrane, most archaeans have a cell wall. This is a tough outer covering that lies outside the cell membrane. The toughness of the wall comes from its unique structure. The surface is covered by proteins that form a rigid layer somewhat like chain mail, an arrangement not seen in other cells. It is this feature that helps them to survive in extreme environments. Some archaeans have a long whip-like structure sticking out of their cell. This is a flagellum, and they use it to move around.

How Do Archaeans Differ from Bacteria?

For a long time, archaeans were not identified as a separate type of organism because they looked just like bacteria. It was not until the genetic material was analyzed that scientists realized that bacteria and archaeans were very different. Both consist of a single cell, with a cell membrane and a cell wall, but the composition of the cell wall is different. Many bacteria move around using a long flagellum. Some archaeans have a flagellum, too, although the majority do not.

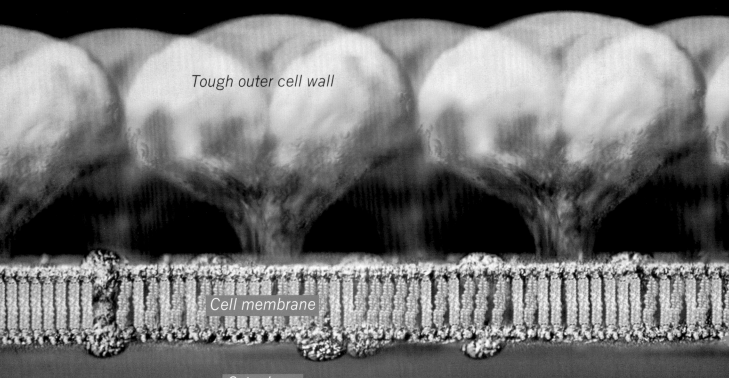

An illustration of an archaean cell wall and membrane. The cell has a layer of tough proteins anchored in the cell membrane. This tough exterior allows archaeans to live in extreme environments.

Tough outer cell wall

Cell membrane

Cytoplasm

The Importance of RNA

Living organisms contain two types of nucleic acids, DNA and RNA. Most of the DNA is found in the nucleus of eukaryotes, while in the prokaryotes most occurs in a single large loop in the cytoplasm. The information locked up in DNA is used to control the functioning of the cell. DNA is a huge molecule made up of two strands that are joined together and twisted into a spiral. It's called a double helix. The second nucleic acid is RNA, which is a single-stranded molecule. There are three types of RNA. One acts as a messenger carrying information from the DNA to the ribosome, the organelle that is responsible for manufacturing proteins. The ribosome is formed from another type of RNA called ribosomal RNA. A third type of RNA, called transfer RNA, picks up amino acids in the cytoplasm and carries them to the ribosome, where they are joined together to form proteins.

Ribosomal RNA has proved to be very important when studying organisms such as those classified as Archaea. When Carl Woese analyzed the RNA, he found it to have more in common with eukaryotes than with bacteria. This led him to suggest that eukaryotes and archaeans had a common ancestor.

All Sorts of Shapes

Bacteria come in a range of shapes, and originally they were classified according to their shape—rods, spheres, and spirals, for example. Archaeans also come in a range of shapes, some of which are similar to those of bacteria. For example, there are rods, spheres, and spirals, which all adds to the confusion between these two groups of organisms. Some archaeans, however, have irregular shapes that are not seen in other organisms. These unusual shapes include thin slivers, very long rod shapes, flat square shapes, triangular shapes, and rectangular rod shapes. Some species of archaeans exist as groups of cells held together with a fine web of filaments forming biofilms and mats.

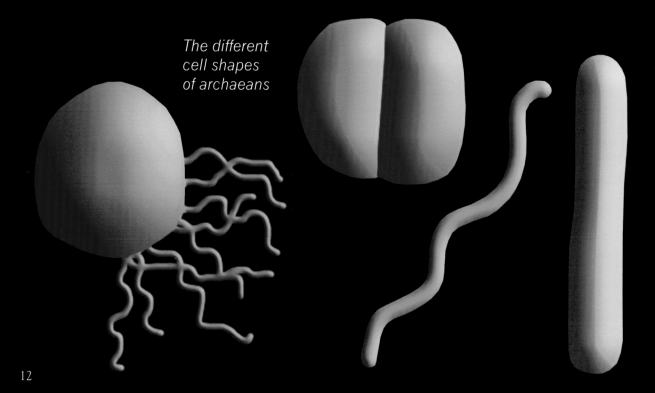

The different cell shapes of archaeans

How Archaeans Feed: Autotrophs and Heterotrophs

Archaeans feed in many different ways. Some can make their own food, while others have to find a ready-made source of food.

Autotrophs are organisms that are self-feeders—that is, they can make their own food from simple inorganic compounds such as carbon dioxide and water. The best-known autotrophs are probably the plants. Plants can make their own food because they contain a green pigment called chlorophyll that can trap light energy. The energy from sunlight is used to combine carbon dioxide and water to make carbohydrates, such as starch and sugar. The gas oxygen is produced as a waste. Some bacteria and archaeans are autotrophs, too. There are archaeans that can use light, while others produce their own food using other sources of energy, such as hydrogen.

Heterotrophs are consumers, which means that they have to eat a ready-made source of food. There are many different types of consumers, the best known being animals. Most animals eat liquid or solid food containing organic compounds. Organic compounds are those that have been made by living organisms—for example, carbohydrates, fats, and proteins. Not surprisingly, there are heterotrophic archaeans too, some of which use methane as their ready-made food source.

Saprophytes are organisms that obtain their food by feeding on dead and decaying matter. Many archaeans, bacteria, and fungi are saprotrophs. They play an essential role in decomposition and the recycling of nutrients.

A colored scanning electron micrograph (SEM) of the archaean Methanosarcina mazei. *These archaeans digest decaying organic matter, and are found in lake sediments, garbage dumps, and also in the intestines of some mammals and insects.*

Living with Oxygen or without Oxygen

Most familiar organisms need oxygen to survive. This is because oxygen is an essential part of the process of respiration. In single-celled organisms such as bacteria and archaeans, oxygen passes directly from the environment across the cell membrane into the cell.

Respiration is a chemical process that takes place inside cells, where large energy-rich molecules such as glucose are broken down to release energy. This energy is then used by the rest of the cell. There are two types of respiration, aerobic respiration, which uses oxygen, and anaerobic respiration, which does not.

LITHOTROPHS: THE STONE-EATERS

Many archaeans are stone-eaters—or to give them their proper name, lithotrophs (lith-o-trofs)—because they get energy from inorganic chemicals (chemicals that are not made by living things), such as ammonia and hydrogen sulfide. In the process of archaeans' breaking down these chemicals, valuable nutrients are released that can be used by other organisms, especially plants. For this reason, biologists believe that these organisms are involved in many nutrient cycles in nature—for example the cycling of sulfur, nitrogen, and carbon—as well as the process of soil formation.

PHOTOSYNTHESIZING ARCHAEANS

One group of archaeans, called haloarchaea, have two types of pigment in their cell membranes that allow them to trap and use light energy, just like plants. But that's where the similarity ends, as their method of synthesizing food using light energy is completely different from that of plants. In addition, haloarchaeans have pigments that detect light and cause the cell to swim toward red light, which is the color of light used by the photosynthesis pigment. Finally, the haloarchaea contain pigments that protect the cell from harmful ultraviolet light from the Sun. These pigments are visible as an orange-red color when there are large numbers of cells together.

Salt can be mined from ponds, built along coastlines, which are filled with seawater. The water evaporates, leaving the salt behind. These salt ponds are one of the habitats where haloarchaea can be found. The orange-red of the salt ponds is due to the coloration of the archaeans and bacteria in the ponds.

Respiration is a very complex process that involves many small steps. The final products of aerobic respiration are carbon dioxide, water, and energy.

For many archaeans, however, oxygen is a killer. So they live in places where there is no oxygen, such as deep in the ground, or in deep water. They still need to respire to obtain energy, so they respire anaerobically—that is, without oxygen. They use nitrate or sulphate molecules instead of oxygen. Their energy sources are different, too, often relying on hydrogen or hydrogen sulphide, and the products of respiration include methane, lactic acid, and ethanol.

Binary Fission: How Archaeans Reproduce

Archaeans reproduce asexually—that is, they make exact copies of themselves. Most do this by dividing in half in a process called binary fission. First the cell grows to full size and makes copies of its genetic material. Then the cell divides into two by forming a new wall across the middle. The two daughter cells are identical to each other and to the parent cell. A few archaeans produce buds that break off and grow into new cells. For example, *Thermofilum pendens* produces an enlargement at one end of the long, thin cell that makes the cell look like a golf club. The enlargement breaks off to form a new cell. Under ideal conditions an archaean can grow and divide every 20 minutes, so they have the potential to increase in number very quickly.

Unlike many other organisms, archaeans are not known to reproduce sexually, so there is no mixing of the genetic material. The two cells produced by binary fission are genetically identical.

Artwork Showing Binary Fission

A fully grown cell

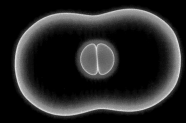

The cell makes copies of its genetic material.

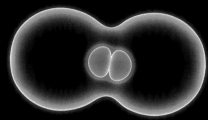

The cell is ready to divide.

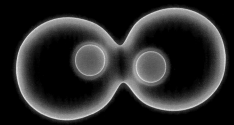

The cell forms a cell wall across the middle.

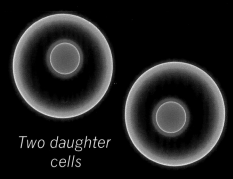

Two daughter cells

Making Mining Waste Dangerous

When minerals such as copper are mined, there is a lot of waste called spoil. This is usually dumped beside the mine, where it is exposed to sunlight and rain. Often the spoil is rich in sulfur-containing substances called pyrites. When these substances are exposed to the air and water, they react to form sulphates, which dissolve in water to form sulfuric acid. The result is an outflow of acidic water from the mine. The presence of the sulfur-compounds makes the water bright red or orange. Few organisms can survive in such a harsh acidic environment, apart from archaeans. Their presence makes matters worse, because they speed up the release of the sulfur when they feed on the energy-rich pyrites. When this acidic water enters local streams and rivers it disrupts the aquatic environment by changing the pH of the water, often killing aquatic animals. Acid mine drainage is particularly common in abandoned mines such as the copper mines of Cornwall, United Kingdom, and the coal mines of Pennsylvania. The only way to tackle this acidic pollution is to neutralize the acidity with alkaline limestone.

A river colored orange and contaminated by highly acidic leachate (water contaminated with spoil) from the disused Wheal Jane Tin Mine in Cornwall, United Kingdom.

Where Do You Find Archaeans?

Archaeans have a reputation for living in very nasty habitats, such as the near-boiling waters of the hot springs of Yellowstone Park. They also live deep in oil wells, in the dark crushing pressure of the ocean floor, in scalding water, in very salty water, and in rock miles beneath the ground. Scientists are also discovering them in less extreme habitats such as ocean water, soil, compost piles, and lake water, where they live alongside bacteria and many other organisms.

Now that scientists know that archaeans exist, they are finding them in a wide range of environments, such as water and soil. In fact, they may turn out to be one of the most common organisms on Earth. They are even found living inside other organisms, including humans.

An archaean that lives in a nasty habitat is called an extremophile (ek-streem-o-file) meaning "extreme-loving." There are many different kinds of extremophiles, including acid-loving, salt-loving, and heat-loving archaeans. They are shown here.

NAMES FOR EXTREMOPHILES

NAME	PRONUNCIATION	MEANING	HABITAT
Acidophile	a-sid-o-file	Acid-loving	pH less than 2
Alkaliphile	al-ka-li-file	Alkaline-loving	pH greater than 7
Barophile	bar-o-file	Pressure-loving	Grow under high pressure deep in the ocean
Halophile	ha-lo-file	Salt-loving	Salty habitats with much more salt than seawater
Psychrophile	sy-kro-file	Cold-loving	Temperatures less than 45°F (7°C)
Mesophile	me-so-file	Middle-loving	Temperatures between 45 and 113°F (7 and 45°C)
Thermophile	ther-mo-file	Heat-loving	Temperatures between 113 and 176°F (45°C and 80°C)
Hyperthermophile	hy-per-ther-mo-file	High heat-loving	Temperatures greater than 176°F (80°C)

Collecting Samples

The archaeans in hot springs and deep-sea hydrothermal vents were discovered by collecting samples from these locations. A scientist dips a jar into the water, breaks off a chunk of a black smoker, or scrapes the surface of a rock. The samples are looked at under a microscope to locate cells. Then scientists try to find the right conditions for the cells to grow in the laboratory. This can be difficult, since the cells may grow at high temperatures, in acid, at high pressure, and without oxygen. Once the cells are growing in the laboratory, they can be studied in detail and given a name and description.

Sampling for archaeans may sound simple on paper, but in practice it can be difficult. When collecting samples near hot springs and mud pools, researchers must be wearing protective gear to prevent hot, acidic water from harming them or doing damage to their equipment. Collecting from the deepest seabeds many miles below the surface is even more difficult. Deep-sea hydrothermal vents are reached using either a deep-ocean submersible or a remotely operated vehicle (ROV) that has been designed to cope with the immense pressure of deep water. Samples are collected using robotic manipulator arms operated by the pilot.

Searching for DNA

More recently, new types of archaeans have been found using environmental DNA sampling. Scientists take samples from ocean water or soil and use the methods similar to those used by crime labs to find DNA. They look for specific DNA sequences that they know belong to Archaea. Once they find that DNA, they look at it in detail. Using this method, scientists can discover how common archaeans are, what groups they belong to, and roughly how many species there might be. They cannot find out exactly what species are there, because they do not collect cells, only the DNA. This method has been used to study archaeans in ocean water, in the mud at the bottom of the ocean, in soil, and even in compost. These studies have increased our knowledge of where archaeans live and have given us a hint that they are important for the ecology of the planet.

Researchers aboard a deep-sea submersible prepare to collect samples of extremophiles living miles below the ocean surface.

Deep underground in a cave system, a scientist collects rock samples to study for bacteria and archaeans.

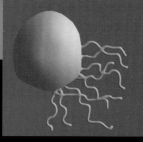
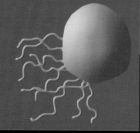

CHAPTER TWO

THE SULFUR-LOVERS

One of the archaeans that Thomas Brock discovered in the hot springs at Yellowstone Park is called *Sulfolobus* (sul-fo-lob-us), meaning "sulfur pod." It lives at temperatures up to 194°F (90°C), which is just below the boiling point of water, and in water as acidic as stomach acid, which is about pH 2–3.

Extremely Adapted

Sulfolobus is typical of many of the archaeans that belong to the phylum Crenarchaeota. These archaeans live in very hot, acidic water, and they need sulfur to live. They tend to be found in sulfur-rich environments such as hot springs and around hydrothermal vents on the seabed. Most are anaerobic, but there are some aerobic examples, too.

The phylum Crenarchaeota is made up of a single class that is divided into four orders. These orders are shown in the chart on page 22.

Life in Hot Springs

Imagine life in boiling water! This is what archaeans and other hot-spring organisms experience on a daily basis. Organisms that live in hot springs need special adaptations. Heat is the first problem. Most living organisms are adapted to grow and reproduce between 32 and 122°F (0 and 50°C). Few environments on Earth are hotter than this for long periods of time.

Special Proteins

Why is high temperature a problem? Living organisms contain proteins, which are large molecules that have an important role in the cell. For example, they help hold the cell membrane together, and they form enzymes, the chemicals that speed up the reactions that take place in cells. High temperature permanently changes the shape of a protein by breaking the chemical bonds that hold it in shape. For example, when an egg is fried, the egg white (a protein) goes from gooey clear to solid white. Proteins cannot do their jobs in the cell if they do not have the correct shape. An organism living in water at 176°F (80°C) must have proteins adapted to the high temperature.

Why do hyperthermophiles not fry like an egg? They have proteins that are either more tightly wound up with more chemical bonds holding them in shape, or they have stronger bonds holding them together. Having more or stronger bonds holds the protein's shape at high temperatures.

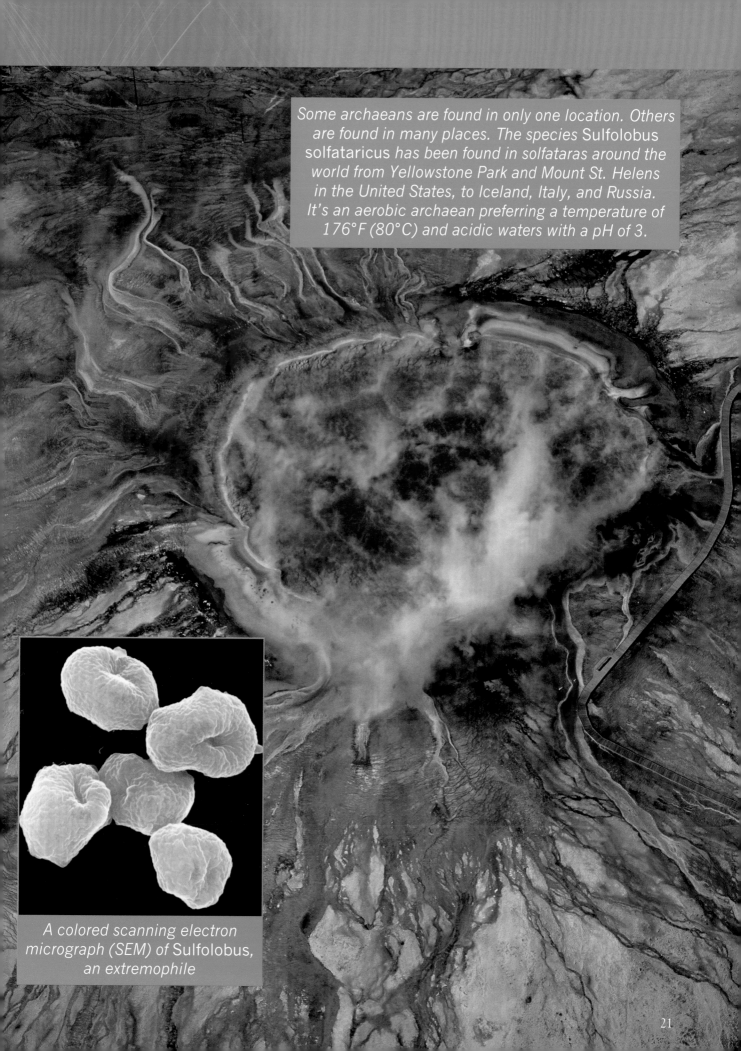

Some archaeans are found in only one location. Others are found in many places. The species Sulfolobus solfataricus *has been found in solfataras around the world from Yellowstone Park and Mount St. Helens in the United States, to Iceland, Italy, and Russia. It's an aerobic archaean preferring a temperature of 176°F (80°C) and acidic waters with a pH of 3.*

A colored scanning electron micrograph (SEM) of Sulfolobus, *an extremophile*

THE FOUR ORDERS OF THE PHYLUM CRENARCHAEOTA

ORDER

Thermoproteales Example species: *Thermofilum pendens*

These are tiny (less than 0.3 micrometers long), rod-shaped cells that live in neutral waters (pH 7) and are mostly anaerobic, meaning they are able to live without oxygen. Scientists think these are the oldest Crenarchaeota.

Caldisphaerales Example species: *Caldisphaera lagunensis*

This is a new order created in 2003 with the discovery of *Caldisphaera lagunensis* in a hot spring on the side of a volcano (Mt. Maquiling) in the Philippines. It has tiny round cells, which range from 0.8–1.1 micrometers in diameter. They prefer a temperature of about 158°F (70°C), so they are thermophiles, and they live best at a pH of 3.5–4.0, so they are also acidophiles. They are anaerobic and get their energy from organic compounds in their environment. Instead of producing carbon dioxide as a waste, they produce hydrogen sulfide, a poisonous gas that smells like rotten eggs.

Desulfurococcales Example species: *Pyrolobus fumarii*

These are small, round cells that live in neutral water of about pH 7, and they are all hyperthermophiles, living in waters at more than 176°F (80°C). They are found in many different hot habitats such as deep-sea hydrothermal vents and hot springs.

Sulfolobales

Example species: *Sulfolobus solfataricus*

These are small, spherical cells that live in acidic hot springs. The species in this order include lithotrophs that need sulfur and species that get energy from organic compounds.

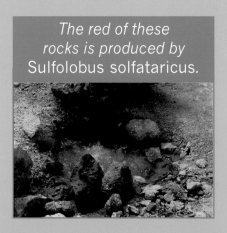

The red of these rocks is produced by Sulfolobus solfataricus.

Coping with Acid

Some of the hot springs are acidic, too, so not only do archaeans have to cope with high temperatures, but they have to be able to withstand the acid—double the trouble for the archaeans.

What's so bad about living in acid? Acid does two things. Like heat, acid changes the shapes of proteins so they don't work. Acid also breaks apart molecules by breaking bonds that even heat cannot break. Most organisms in acid will start to fall apart because of this. So how do archaeans survive in acid? They do two things. First, these cells control their internal pH, keeping it at an acceptable level, at about a neutral pH of 7. They achieve this by pumping out excess acid from the cell using special proteins in the cell membrane. Second, the cells have resistant cell membranes. There are molecules in their cell membranes with strong bonds that are resistant to the effects of acids. Scientists believe that this is one reason that acids do not destroy the cells.

THERMOFILUM PENDENS

Domain:	Archaea
Phylum:	Crenarchaeota
Class:	Thermoprotei
Order:	Thermoproteales
Family:	Thermoproteaceae
Genus:	*Thermofilum*
Species:	*Thermofilum pendens*

Notice the yellow sulfur and the absence of liquid water in this solfatara.

CASE STUDY

Thermofilum pendens: A Dependent Species

Thermofilum pendens (ther-mah-fil-um pend-enz), meaning "dependent hot filament," was first collected from a solfatara in Iceland in 1983. A solfatara is an opening in Earth's crust that emits steam and other gases that are rich in sulfur. It is like a hot spring, but without liquid water, only steam. *Thermofilum pendens* is a long, hair-like cell that grows without oxygen and needs sulfur just as we need oxygen. It feeds on proteins from its environment. Interestingly, it is only ever found living with a second species, called *Thermoproteus tenax*, and scientists believe that *Thermofilum pendens* needs molecules made by *Thermoproteus tenax* that it cannot make by itself. The two species are always found together. This is why scientists gave it the name *pendens*, meaning "dependent."

New Life at the Bottom of the Ocean

In 1977, scientists exploring the deep ocean east of the Galápagos Islands made a startling discovery. They were exploring the seabed at depths of 6,560 feet (2,000 meters), in a deep water submersible when they discovered gaps in the rocks where super-hot (750°F/399°C), mineral-rich water gushed out, just like a geyser. Living around these deep-sea hydrothermal vents was an amazing array of life-forms never seen before, including huge clams and giant tube worms more than nine feet (2.7 meters) long. These animals were surviving in dark, cold water, under extremely high pressure. There were no plants, so these animals were relying on autotrophic bacteria that were feeding on the minerals in the water. At the time, scientists did not know about archaeans, but now we know that archaeans are common around these vents, too, feeding on iron sulphide and other minerals.

Giant tube worms are anchored on the seabed beside a hydrothermal vent.

Living in a Black Smoker

Pyrolobus fumarii (pi-ro-lo-bus few-mar-ee-ee) was discovered in 1997 on the wall of the chimney of a black smoker at a depth of 2.3 miles (3.7 kilometers) on the Mid-Atlantic Ridge. A black smoker is a kind of underwater hot spring. The heated water has minerals dissolved in it that turn to solid black particles when they hit the cold ocean water. The black minerals collect at the opening of the spring and form tall chimneys. *Pyrolobus* grows best at a temperature of 223°F (106°C) and can even grow at a temperature of 235°F (113°C). Because of the extreme pressure, the waters at this depth are hotter than boiling water on land. At the time, *Pyrolobus* was living in the hottest temperature known for a living organism. It also lived at low oxygen levels, in mildly acidic waters, where it survived a pressure 247 times the air pressure at sea level. *Pyrolobus* is a lithotroph, using hydrogen gas as an energy source. It releases poisonous ammonia and hydrogen sulfide as waste.

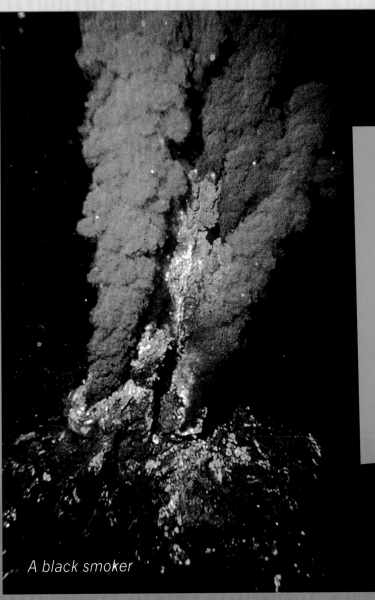

A black smoker

DID LIFE BEGIN IN A HYDROTHERMAL VENT?

Many scientists think it is possible that life may have started in hydrothermal vents, rather than in shallow warm seawater. There are several reasons for this. First, the heat is a source of energy to make the molecules necessary for life. Second, the minerals coming from the heated water can speed up the formation of the molecules of life. Finally, early Earth was constantly being hit by meteorites, so life deep in the sea was probably safer than on the surface.

Ignicoccus hospitalis: Living Together

Ignicoccus hospitalis (ig-ni-kah-kus hah-spit-al-is), meaning "hospitable rock berry," was discovered in 2002 in a hydrothermal vent off the coast of Iceland. It is an anaerobic archaean that uses sulfur in its respiration the way humans use oxygen. The cells are round, about one micrometer in diameter, and unusual because they have two membranes with a space between them that contains structures. Scientists have wondered whether *Ignicoccus* might show how the nucleus in eukaryotes could have evolved, since the inner membrane contains the genetic material and has parts of the cell between it and the outer membrane. *Ignicoccus* also has an external archaean parasite, *Nanoarchaeum equitans*. The smaller *Nanoarchaeum* lacks some enzymes needed to manufacture essential substances, so it has to get them from its larger partner.

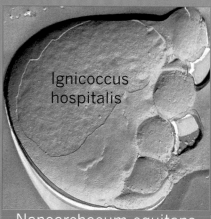

Ignicoccus hospitalis

Nanoarchaeum equitans

IGNICOCCUS HOSPITALIS

Domain:	Archaea
Phylum:	Crenarchaeota
Class:	Thermoprotei
Order:	Desulfurococcales
Family:	Pyrodictiaceae
Genus:	*Ignicoccus*
Species:	*Ignicoccus hospitalis*

THE HEAT RECORD

An archaean, Strain 121, is able to survive the highest temperature of any living thing, 250°F (121°C). The record temperature is how it got its name. This temperature is of interest because hospitals and scientists use steam and pressure in steel chambers called autoclaves to kill bacteria on their instruments. The temperature in an autoclave reaches 250°F (121°C). Luckily Strain 121 does not cause disease, but if it can survive an autoclave, maybe other less friendly organisms can also.

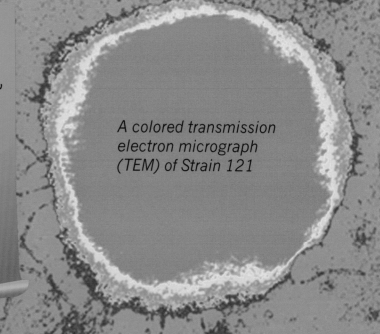

A colored transmission electron micrograph (TEM) of Strain 121

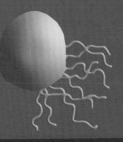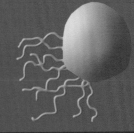

CHAPTER THREE

THE RECYCLERS

Not all archaeans live in extreme environments. As biologists carry out more environmental sampling of DNA, they are finding that these organisms are far more widespread than previously thought. Many make up the plankton in the surface waters of the oceans. Some live under the ice in Antarctica. Others are found in soil, where they have a critical role to play in the recycling of some of the most important minerals, including carbon, nitrogen, and sulfur.

A Phylum of Their Own?

The recycling archaeans of the newly proposed phylum Thaumarchaeota were once classified within phylum Crenarchaeota, but analysis of their DNA has made many scientists feel that they should have their own phylum.

Thaumarchaeota has one class and two orders: Nitrosopumilales and Cenarchaeales.

Cenarchaeum symbiosum *lives inside a sponge,* Axinella, *that is found in 33–66 feet (10–20 m) of water off the coast of California. It prefers a temperature of about 50°F (10°C). The cells are rod-shaped, 0.8 micrometers long, and 0.5 micrometers wide. The DNA of this species shows it to be closely related to archaeans that have been found by DNA sampling in seawater.*

CASE STUDY

Preparing to Find Life in the Solar System

Dr. Alison Murray is a research biologist who studies archaeans and bacteria in the waters off Antarctica by collecting their DNA. The water temperature is 28.8°F (−1.8°C). There are so many archaeans that they make up 20 percent of the prokaryotes found in these waters. It is likely that similar numbers of archaeans exist in other oceans.

Dr. Murray participates in a NASA research program that is investigating the possibility of life existing in bodies of water elsewhere in the solar system. Scientists believe it is possible that the moons of some planets, such as Saturn's Titan and Jupiter's Europa, may contain large bodies of water below their surfaces. If there is life in very cold lakes beneath the ice of Antarctica, could there be life on these moons? Scientists study life in Antarctica and other cold places on Earth to learn what to look for to find life when a spacecraft can be sent to explore these distant moons.

Europa

Titan

Cycling Nitrogen

All living things need nitrogen because it is one of the building blocks of proteins. Nitrogen is an abundant element, and nitrogen gas makes up almost 80 percent of Earth's atmosphere. The problem is that very few organisms can deal with nitrogen in its gaseous form. Plants, for example, need nitrogen in the form of ammonium or nitrates, which they can take up through their roots. Somehow nitrogen gas (N_2) has to be converted to a form they can use. This is achieved through the action of bacteria and archaeans. There are different stages in the nitrogen cycle. Some bacteria and archaeans are found living in the roots of plants where they combine nitrogen gas with hydrogen to make ammonium that the plants use. Other archaeans live in the soil, where they help in the breakdown of organic matter that is rich in nitrogen and convert it to nitrates. There is a third group of microorganisms that take nitrates in the soil and convert them back into nitrogen gas, so completing the cycle.

The Nitrogen Cycle

Bacteria and archaeans turn nitrogen gas in the air into nitrates in the soil.

Plants take up nitrates from the soil through their roots. Bacteria and archaeans living in the roots of some plants turn nitrogen into ammonium, which is used by the plant to make protein.

Some species of bacteria and archaeans turn nitrates back into nitrogen gas.

Animals get their nitrogen from eating either plants or other animals. Animal waste is turned back into nitrates by bacteria and archaea in the soil.

CASE STUDY

Nitrosopumilus maritimus: A Key Player

Nitrosopumilus maritimus was discovered in mud at the bottom of a tank at the Seattle Aquarium in 2005. Scientists knew there were many Crenarchaeota living in the oceans because they had found their DNA. This was the first Crenarchaeota to be grown in the laboratory. *Nitrosopumilus maritimus* is a particularly small example, just 0.2 micrometers in diameter, but it has a critical role to play in the ocean, where it helps convert ammonia to nitrate, a key step in the nitrogen cycle.

CHAPTER FOUR

THE METHANE-MAKERS
AND OTHER EURYARCHAEOTA

A methanogen (meth-an-o-jen), meaning "methane-maker," does what its name would suggest—it produces methane—and thus forms an important group of archaeans.

The Making of Methane

Methane is a small molecule that contains carbon and hydrogen. Methanogens release methane as a waste product, much as we release carbon dioxide when we breathe. Methane is a gas that burns in the presence of oxygen to produce carbon dioxide and water. It is the main gas in natural gas, which is used to heat homes and to cook. Most of the world's natural gas was not produced by the action of archaeans, but was formed underground by pressure and heat in the distant past. Now, however, methane is produced all over the planet by archaeans. Archaeans are the only organisms able to do this.

There are many known species of methanogens in the phylum Euryarchaeota. They feed on different food molecules to produce the methane. Often their food molecules are produced by bacteria, and so the archaeans live with bacteria in order to survive. Methanogens cannot survive in oxygen, so they are found in anaerobic environments such as the deep sea, lake and

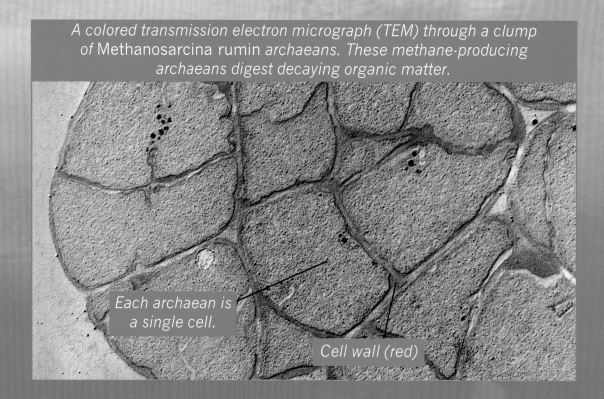

A colored transmission electron micrograph (TEM) through a clump of Methanosarcina rumin archaeans. These methane-producing archaeans digest decaying organic matter.

Each archaean is a single cell.

Cell wall (red)

swamp bottoms, and inside the digestive systems of animals. Methanogens can be thermophiles, mesophiles, or psychrophiles.

There are five orders of methanogens in the Euryarchaeota. Scientists believe that the ability to make methane is a very old trait in archaeans. They think it is possible that all the ancestors of Euryarchaeota once had the ability to make methane. The Euryarchaeota today that do not make methane—the salt-loving and heat-loving forms—have lost that ability.

Methanogens and the Carbon Cycle

Methanogens play a major role in the global carbon cycle, the process by which carbon is taken up by plants and animals and returned to the environment in a never-ending cycle. Carbon dioxide in the atmosphere is taken up by autotrophs including plants, bacteria, and archaeans. The autotrophs are eaten by heterotrophs, such as animals. The process of respiration releases carbon dioxide back to the atmosphere. In addition, the breakdown or decomposition of dead matter releases carbon dioxide and methane back to the atmosphere. Sometimes, dead plants and animals are buried and over millions of years the organic matter is turned into coal, oil, and gas. When fossil fuels are burned, the carbon is released back into the atmosphere as carbon dioxide.

Archaeans and bacteria are important in biodigesters where organic waste is broken down to produce methane and other gases.

Some methanogens can use carbon dioxide as their source of carbon and produce methane. They are also involved in the decomposition or breakdown of organic matter in anaerobic environments, such as in swamps and in mud on the seabed. In the process, they are estimated to produce close to 400 million tons (363 metric tons) of methane per year.

Since methanogens are important players in the carbon cycle, they are especially important for global warming. Methane is a stronger greenhouse gas than carbon dioxide, because each molecule of methane has a greater warming effect than a molecule of carbon dioxide. As a result of human activities, the concentration of methane in the atmosphere has almost tripled in the last 200 years.

Archaeans are also responsible for producing vast quantities of methane trapped in ice crystals at the bottom of the oceans. This trapped methane is important because some people see it as an energy source, while others see it as a global warming threat. Scientists worry that global warming will warm the oceans, which will melt the ice crystals and release the methane into the atmosphere. If this happened, there would be a dramatic increase in global warming. The methane trapped at the ocean bottom is also being considered as a possible energy source—although burning it will release greenhouse gases.

METHANE CONTROL

As methane levels in the atmosphere rise, scientists are looking more closely at archaeans to find ways of reducing the levels. Some scientists are looking for ways to reduce the amount of methane produced by archaeans in the digestive systems of cattle partly as a way to slow global warming. This may be possible by altering the diet of the cattle.

An ice sample from Antarctica from a depth of 768 feet (234 m). The ice will be tested for its methane content by analyzing the air pockets trapped in the ice.

Our Own Personal Archaeans

Our guts are full of prokaryotes such as archaeans and bacteria that help us digest our food. They are particularly common in the large intestine, where they help break down the fiber in food. Humans lack enzymes that can break down fiber, so these microorganisms do the job for us. The main archaean in the human digestive system is called *Methanobrevibacter smithii* (meth-an-o-brev-i-bak-ter smith-ee-ee), meaning "Smith's short methane-making rod." Up to 10 percent of the prokaryotes in the large intestine belong to this species.

This archaean has an interesting relationship with bacteria. Bacteria produce hydrogen gas as a waste product, and this is used by *Methanobrevibacter smithii* as food. In fact, the hydrogen is a poison to the bacteria, so when *Methanobrevibacter smithii* removes it, the bacteria are able to continue to grow and reproduce. These relationships are an example of mutualism—organisms living together and all helping each other. In this case the mutualism involves bacteria, an archaean, and humans. Each of the species involved in the relationship benefits.

Different species of archaeans have been collected from cows, horses, geese, and sheep, too. Two other species of *Methanobrevibacter* have been collected from the digestive system of a termite from Michigan. Another methanogen called *Methanomicrococcus blatticola* (meth-an-o-meye-kro-kah-kus blat-i-co-la), meaning "methane-making tiny berry from the cockroach," was collected from the digestive system of the palmetto cockroach, which is common in the United States. Methanogens were observed in the intestine of the cockroach by shining ultraviolet light on them. Methanogens have a molecule that emits a pale blue light (fluorescence) under ultraviolet light, so they can be detected using this method. The scientists collected the cells and studied them. They are small irregular cells about one micrometer in diameter. They feed on methanol and hydrogen gas released by bacteria in the digestive system of the cockroach.

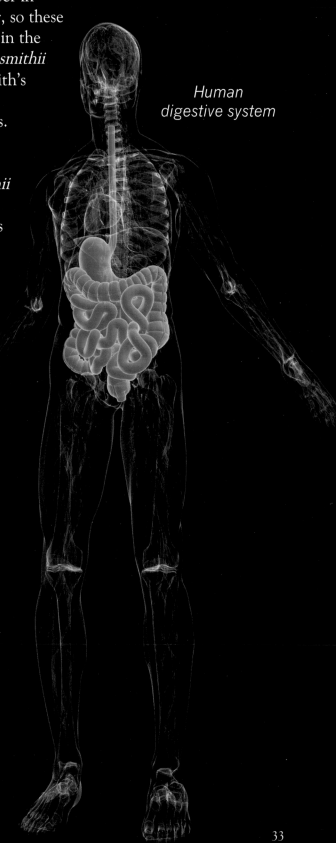

Human digestive system

CASE STUDY

Methanococcus aeolicus: Windy Archaeans

Methanococcus aeolicus (meth-an-o-kah-kus ay-ol-ic-us), meaning "methane-making berry from the Aeolian islands," is an archaean that seems to be an important species in seafloor sediments. It was named after the Aeolian Islands, the volcanic islands north of Sicily, where the species was first collected. Aeolus was the Greek god of wind. It was first found in shallow water, but it has since been found in deeper waters (3,120 feet/951 m) off the coast of Japan. This species has proved to be very useful in genetic engineering, as some of its enzymes have been used as "molecular scissors" to chop lengths of DNA into shorter fragments.

METHANOCOCCUS AEOLICUS

Domain:	Archaea
Phylum:	Euryarchaeota
Class:	Methanococci
Order:	Methanococcales
Family:	Methanococcaceae
Genus:	*Methanococcus*
Species:	*Methanococcus aeolicus*

Methanolobus zinderi (meth-an-o-lob-us zin-der-eye), meaning "Zinder's methane-making pod," was collected from water from a coal deposit 3,038 feet (926 m) underground in Louisiana. They are irregular cells about one micrometer in diameter. They grow best at 104–122°F (40–50°C). Among other substances, it eats methanol, an alcohol that is poisonous to humans. The DNA of another archaean has been collected from a coal deposit in Illinois. Scientists believe that archaeans are the last step in breaking down coal to produce methane. Bacteria begin the process, and archaeans feed on the waste molecules released by bacteria and make methane.

Life in Hot Oil Deposits

Oil forms deep in the ground. Amazingly, some archaeans from the Euryarchaeota have discovered these deposits and use them as a source of food. Crude oil is a mix of many different substances that contain carbon, hydrogen, and oxygen, so it is an energy and carbon-rich food. Scientists were surprised to learn that archaeans could feed on crude oil, while living in an oxygen-free environment. Until this discovery, scientists believed that oil could only be used as food by microorganisms living in oxygen. Archaeans may even be responsible for producing some of the world's natural gas, since one of the waste products of eating oil is natural gas. In the future it may be possible to extract enzymes that could be used to help clean up underground water supplies that have been contaminated by oil.

C A S E   S T U D Y

Archaeoglobus fulgidus: Oil- and Hydrogen-eaters

Archaeoglobus fulgidus (ar-kee-o-glob-us ful-jid-us), meaning "shining ancient sphere," are lumpy spheres with a flagellum that allows them to move. They grow best at 181°F (83°C). They eat organic molecules, including oil, or live on inorganic molecules such as hydrogen gas. Like their close relatives, they use sulfur compounds the way we use oxygen and must have an oxygen-free environment to live. This species was first found at a hydrothermal vent near the island of Volcano in Italy, but they also live in deposits of oil deep under the seabed. Being closer to Earth's hot core, the temperature here is nearly 212°F (100°C).

ARCHAEOGLOBUS FULGIDUS

Domain: Archaea
Phylum: Euryarchaeota
Class: Archaeoglobi
Order: Archaeoglobales
Family: Archaeoglobaceae
Genus: *Archaeoglobus*
Species: *Archaeoglobus fulgidus*

Drilling for oil deep below the ocean

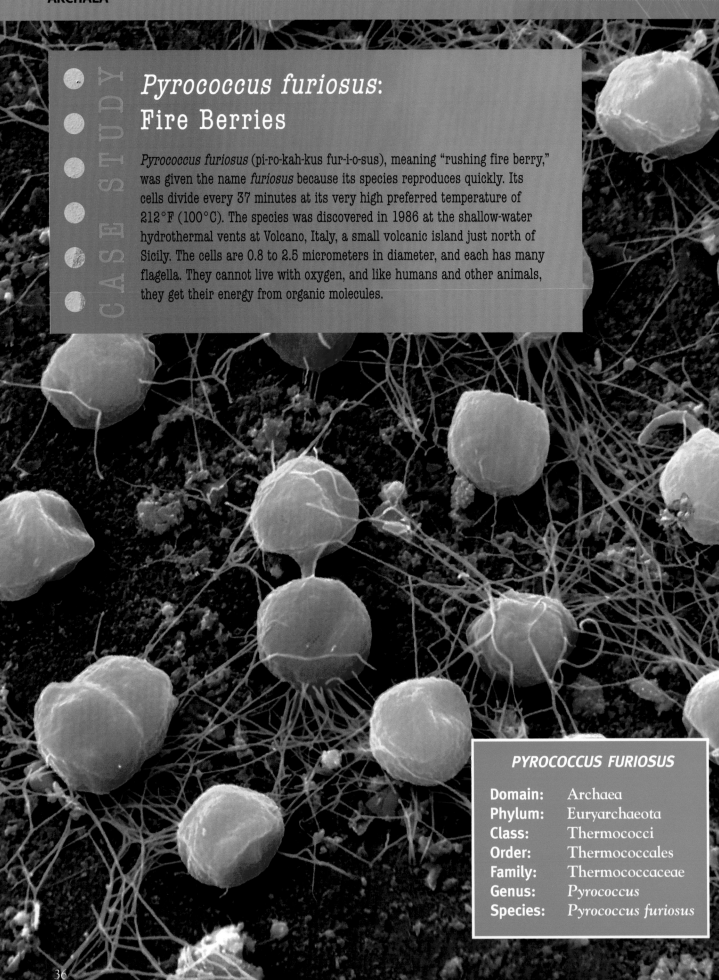

Pyrococcus furiosus:
Fire Berries

Pyrococcus furiosus (pi-ro-kah-kus fur-i-o-sus), meaning "rushing fire berry," was given the name *furiosus* because its species reproduces quickly. Its cells divide every 37 minutes at its very high preferred temperature of 212°F (100°C). The species was discovered in 1986 at the shallow-water hydrothermal vents at Volcano, Italy, a small volcanic island just north of Sicily. The cells are 0.8 to 2.5 micrometers in diameter, and each has many flagella. They cannot live with oxygen, and like humans and other animals, they get their energy from organic molecules.

PYROCOCCUS FURIOSUS

Domain:	Archaea
Phylum:	Euryarchaeota
Class:	Thermococci
Order:	Thermococcales
Family:	Thermococcaceae
Genus:	*Pyrococcus*
Species:	*Pyrococcus furiosus*

The Acid-lovers

Some of the thermophilic Euryarchaeota are acid-lovers that grow best at a pH of 2 or lower. The most acid-living archaeans of them all are *Picrophilus*, which have been collected from solfataras in northern Japan. These amazing archaeans grow best at a pH of 0.6, but they can even grow at pH 0. It's hard to imagine just how acidic that is, but these archaeans could grow in concentrated acid from the laboratory or in battery acid if it was hot enough. If you spill this concentrated acid, it burns straight through your clothes, so imagine how tough an organism has to be, not just to survive, but grow and reproduce in such extreme conditions.

Another acid-lover is *Thermoplasma acidophilum*, which was discovered in hot coal waste by a student of Thomas Brock in 1970, before archaeans were known about. Its preferred pH is between 1 and 2. It has also been found in solfataras. It grows best at a temperature of 140°F (60°C). It is a scavenger, feeding on molecules made by other organisms. Scientists have studied many aspects of this species to understand how it survives at high temperatures and high acidity.

An Archaean That Eats Iron

Sometimes it seems that archaeans have adapted to get their energy from almost anything that is available. *Ferroplasma acidophilum*, meaning "acid-loving iron form," eats iron. It was isolated from an industrial operation that was extracting gold from rock. It has also been found in the waste from mining operations. It prefers a pH of 1.7 and temperatures of about 95°F (35°C). The cells are irregular, 1–3 micrometers long, and 0.3–1.0 micrometer wide. This species reproduces by producing little buds that break off the main cell. Scientists think that iron may have been a more common food for cells in the early history of life.

This photograph illustrates how tough archaeans have to be to live in acid. Here, metal from scrap cars is being recycled by being dissolved in large vats of acid to extract titanium oxide.

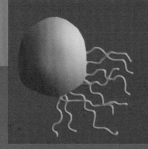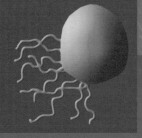

CHAPTER FIVE

THE SALT-LOVERS

The salt-lovers, or halophiles, make up a large group within Euryarchaeota. They all live in habitats with salt concentrations greater than that found in seawater. These are called hypersaline habitats. Water cannot dissolve any more salt than about ten times the concentration of seawater.

Very Salty Habitats

Most hypersaline environments are found in lakes. There are examples of salty lakes around the world. The saltiest body of water is the Dead Sea, a very large salt lake in the Middle East that is almost nine times as salty as the ocean. In the United States, the Great Salt Lake is the largest salt lake. Salt lakes are found on all of the other continents, including Antarctica.

Halophiles have also been found in underground salt deposits, which are mined to give us table salt. The other way salt is collected for human use is by evaporating seawater in shallow pools. These pools, or salterns, are typically orange-red in color because of the haloarchaeans living in them. Haloarchaeans have also been found living on fish meat that has been salted to be preserved. Finally, some have been found in very salty water on the ocean floor where hypersaline water collects over the seabed.

The species Halorhabdus utahensis *(hay-lo-rab-dus yu-ta-en-sis), meaning "salt rod from Utah," was collected from the Great Salt Lake in Utah in 2000. Its cells are irregular in shape and have a single flagellum 3–5 micrometers long. They grow best at 122°F (50°C), although this is hotter than their habitat ever reaches. They also grow best at a pH of about 7. They prefer a salinity about eight times as great as seawater. This image shows salt deposits on the beaches of the Great Salt Lake.*

Coping with Salt

Organisms must be adapted to cope with living in a high salt habitat. The internal environment of most cells has about the same salt concentration as seawater. When an organism finds itself in water that has a higher salt content outside its cell membrane than it has inside, water flows out through the cell membrane from the inside of the cell to the outside. The cell will actually dry out. The haloarchaeans counter this by raising the salt concentration inside their cell. This is achieved by importing salt. This results in a high concentration of salts inside the cell, which means that the DNA and proteins of haloarchaeans must be adapted to high salt surroundings, too.

Alkali-lovers

Some salt lakes are alkaline with a pH greater than 7. These lakes are called soda lakes. Living in alkaline conditions causes problems very similar to those facing the archaeans that live in acidic conditions, as the alkalinity damages cells and alters the structure of proteins.

Haloarchaeans that live in soda lakes are either rod-shaped or round. Two species of the genus *Natronococcus* (nay-tron-o-kah-kus), meaning soda berry, were collected from Lake Magadi in Kenya, a soda lake that receives its water mostly from hot springs. One is orange-red in color, and the other is pale brown. They are round and 1–2 micrometers in diameter. They do not have flagella and cannot move. These species grow best at the extremely high pH of 9–9.5. The third species in this genus was found in fermented shrimp food made in Korea called jeotgal. This species prefers a less alkaline habitat, growing best at pH 7.5.

Salt crystals on the shore of the Dead Sea

Brine pools

Water becomes more dense as its salinity increases, so it will sink below water that contains less salt. Water bodies often contain different layers of water that have different salt concentrations, and these layers do not mix. As a result, some lakes have salty water on their bottoms and freshwater on their surface. It also happens in seas, where heavy, very salty water lies on the bottom and normal seawater lies on top without the two layers ever mixing. Often, the bottom layer also has no oxygen because it is separated from the atmosphere by the upper layer.

The archaean *Halorhabdus tiamatea* (hay-lo-rab-dus ti-a-ma-tay-a), meaning "Tiamat's salt rod" (Tiamat was the Mesopotamian goddess of salty water), was collected from a deep-sea brine at a depth of 4,747 feet (1,447 m) in the Red Sea. The temperature was 75°F (24°C), and the salt concentration was seven times the salinity of seawater. The species is unusual among all of the haloarchaeans because it grows best without oxygen. This species also does not have any color, and because its natural habitat is pitch black, it does not need protection from ultraviolet radiation, nor can it get energy from light.

A tunnel in an underground salt mine

Ancient Archaeans

41

Species of *Halococcus* (hay-lo-kah-kus), meaning "salt berry" have been collected from dry rock salt 2,133 feet (650 m) below the ground in a mine in Austria and from other salt mines around the world. The salt in the mine in Austria was formed during the Permian period up to 300 million years ago. Scientists who have discovered archaeans in rock salt cautiously suggest that the cells have survived from that time. They are cautious, because this would be an amazing fact if it were true. They do not know if the cells could have survived by growing and reproducing in pockets of water within the salt, or if they were in some kind of resting state. The possibility of survival of archaeans in rocks over millions of years raises the possibility that there may be similar life-forms beneath the surface on Mars, which has deposits of water beneath its surface.

Haloarcula quadrata: Square Archaeans

Several species of square and even triangular archaeans have been discovered. These are unusual shapes for cells. Cells have more pressure inside them than outside, and so they push out like the air in a balloon. The natural shape for a cell like this is a sphere, or a rounded shape. Cells with sharp corners are difficult to explain. *Haloarcula quadrata* (hay-lo-ar-kew-la kwad-rat-a), meaning "square salt-requiring small box," has cells that are flat squares, orange in color, and can move with one or more flagella. They were collected from brine pools on the Sinai Peninsula, in Egypt.

CASE STUDY

HALOARCULA QUADRATA	
Domain:	Archaea
Phylum:	Euryarchaeota
Class:	Halobacteria
Order:	Halobacteriales
Family:	Halobacteriaceae
Genus:	*Haloarcula*
Species:	*Haloarcula quadrata*

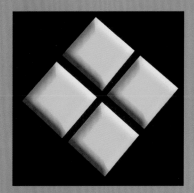

An illustration of Haloarcula quadrata

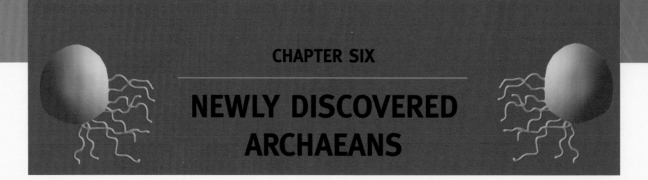

CHAPTER SIX

NEWLY DISCOVERED ARCHAEANS

Although science is only beginning to learn about the vast diversity of species that make up the domain Archaea, most—but not all—newly discovered species usually fit within one of two phyla: the Crenarchaeota and the Euryarchaeota. There are also newly discovered archaeans whose DNA do not fit any of the earlier established or proposed Archaea phyla. They have been placed in a phyla of their own. The Korarchaeota have been collected with DNA sampling, but no cells have been grown. The other is Nanoarchaeota, which right now has just one species as a member!

Korarchaeota: "Young Ancient Things"

These species have only been collected from hot springs and hydrothermal vents using DNA sampling methods. The first sample was found in Obsidian Pool in Yellowstone National Park. Other samples have been found in hot springs in Iceland and Japan, and in deep-sea hydrothermal vents near Iceland and Japan and in the Sea of Cortez, the Pacific Ocean, and the Mediterranean Sea. Although it has not been possible to grow these cells in the laboratory, a cell was isolated and its DNA collected, and scientists are analyzing its DNA. Scientists have looked for Korarchaeota DNA in environments that do not have high temperatures, but they have not been able to find any signs of them. This seems to mean that Korarchaeota only live in high temperature habitats.

Nanoarchaeota: "Very Young Ancient Things"

Nanoarchaeum equitans was discovered in 2002 in a submarine hot spring 348 feet (106 m) below the ocean surface north of Iceland. It lives attached to *Ignicoccus hospitalis*, a Crenarchaeota. *Nanoarchaeum* cannot live without its host *Ignicoccus*, and it is believed to be a parasite. It is a very small, round cell, about 0.4 micrometer in diameter. When scientists looked at the DNA of *Nanoarchaeum*, it did not seem to be related to any of the other groups of archaeans, and so it was put in its own phylum. They discovered that it had a short length of DNA and has lost a number of genes that were found in other archaeans. It can survive because it relies on *Ignicoccus* to make the molecules it needs. This is typical of parasitic species. The researchers that analyzed the DNA felt that *Nanoarchaeum* belonged in its own phylum. But others disagree. When other genes were compared by scientists in 2006, it seemed that *Nanoarchaeum* belonged with the Euryarchaeota. Further studies and the discovery of new species related to *Nanoarchaeum* will provide more information on this important question.

Other researchers have discovered DNA samples that are similar to *Nanoarchaeum* at a submarine vent in the Pacific Ocean, in Obsidian Pool at Yellowstone, and in a hot spring in Russia. There are more species of this interesting phylum out there to be discovered.

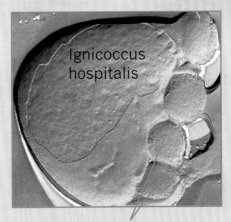

Ignicoccus hospitalis

Nanoarchaeum equitans

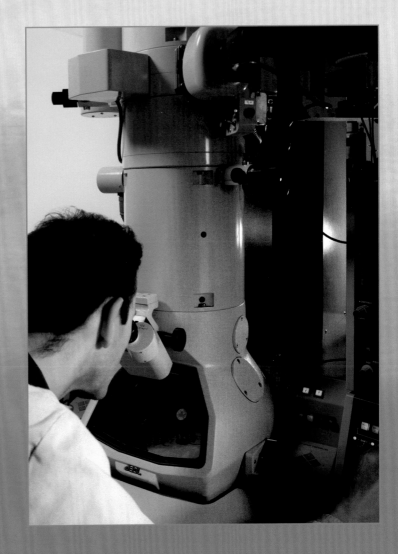

Scientists will continue to search for, study, and classify archaeans. Here, scientists collect samples from hot springs in Iceland (opposite).

A scientist uses a scanning electron microscope to look at samples (right).

Glossary

acid A bitter-tasting, corrosive substance that reacts with a base or alkali to form a salt; acids release hydrogen ions

adaptation A trait of an organism that allows it to live and reproduce in its environment; adaptations are a consequence of evolution by natural selection

aerobic Involving or requiring oxygen

alkali Also called a base; a corrosive substance that reacts with an acid to form a salt; alkaline substances take up hydrogen ions

anaerobic Without oxygen, the opposite of aerobic

black smoker A type of deep-sea hydrothermal vent in which mineral-rich, super-heated water enters cold seawater causing the minerals to become solid; the solid minerals have a black color and collect to form tall narrow chimneys above where the water leaves the ocean bottom

carbon cycle The different places that carbon atoms move on Earth, including the atmosphere, the oceans, organisms, and rocks. Living organisms, including humans, participate in the carbon cycle by using carbon in their bodies

carbon dioxide A chemical compound made of two oxygen atoms bonded to a carbon atom

cell The smallest unit of life

cell membrane The structure separating all cells from the environment around them; the cell membrane is formed of lipids and contains proteins that help the cell communicate with the environment and take in or put out various substances

cell wall A tough protective covering around a cell, outside the cell membrane

chemical bond The attraction between two atoms in a chemical compound that keeps them next to each other

DNA Deoxyribonucleic acid, a complex molecule that is the blueprint for a living thing; it contains all the information for building cells and bodies

DNA sequence The order of the four nucleotides in a gene, or a piece of DNA, or an organism's whole genome, all of its DNA

environmental DNA sampling A method used by scientists to quickly find out the kinds of organisms that live in a habitat by collecting and identifying their DNA, but without identifying particular species

enzyme A molecule in an organism that is key to making chemical reactions happen— for example, breaking down of food molecules in digestion

eukaryote An organism whose cells have a nucleus and other cell parts separated from the rest of the cell by a membrane; plants, animals, fungi, and protists are eukaryotes

extremophile An organism that is able to live in environments with conditions outside of the range of most environments on Earth, such as extreme temperature, acidity, salinity, pressure, radiation, or depth within Earth

flagellum (pl. *flagella*) A whip-like structure extending through the cell membrane of a cell and capable of motion that allows a cell to swim

gene A segment of DNA that carries information

hydrothermal vent An opening in Earth's crust that allows water heated by Earth's magma to leave; hydrothermal vents are found in areas of volcanic activity or where magma is close to Earth's surface; hot springs and geysers are hydrothermal vents and they are also found on the ocean floor

inorganic Describes a chemical compound that does not contain carbon, or that was not made by an organism

lithotroph An organism that gets energy from inorganic compounds

methane A chemical compound made of four hydrogen atoms bonded to one carbon atom

methanogen A prokaryote that produces methane as a waste

micrometer A length equal to one millionth of a meter, or one thousandth of a millimeter

nitrogen cycle The different places that nitrogen atoms move on Earth, including the atmosphere, the oceans, organisms, and soil. The nitrogen cycle is controlled by living organisms, mostly bacteria and archaea

nucleus The structure in a eukaryotic cell where the DNA is kept

organelle A structure in the cell of a eukaryote that has one or more functions and is usually surrounded by a membrane

organic Describes a chemical compound that contains carbon

organism A living thing; can refer to an individual or a species

parasite A relationship between two organisms in which one obtains nourishment from the other, causing it harm

pH A scale that goes from 0 to 14 that describes how acidic or alkaline something is. Values less than 7 are acidic; for example lemon juice, vinegar, stomach acid. Values greater than 7 are alkaline; for example lye and ammonia. A value of 7 is neutral, neither acidic, nor alkaline

photosynthesis The process by which an organism forms organic molecules using the energy of light

phylum One of the levels of classification of organisms, which in order from smallest to largest are species, genus, family, order, class, phylum, kingdom, domain. In plants the phylum is called a division

prokaryote An organism that does not have its DNA enclosed in a nucleus; prokaryotes include the unrelated groups of bacteria and archaea

protein A large molecule made up of subunits called amino acids that are linked together in a chain. Proteins have many functions such as carrying oxygen, forming hair and nails, and functioning as enzymes

sediment The fine particles of matter that settle at the bottom of a water body such as a lake or ocean

soda lake A saline lake that is also alkaline

solfatara An opening in Earth's crust that produces steam, not water, and sulfurous gases

species In sexual organisms, a group of individual organisms that can mate and produce fertile offspring; in asexual organisms a group of individual organisms with very similar characteristics and DNA sequences

termite A small, soft-bodied insect that lives in large, well-organized colonies; termites feed on plant materials with the help of bacteria and archaea in their digestive systems to break down plant fiber

Further Information–Web sites

www.learner.org/courses/biology/units/microb/experts/reysenbach.html
Here is an interview with Anna-Louise Reysenbach, a scientist who studies life in the hot springs at Yellowstone Park.

www.learner.org/courses/biology/units/microb/index.html
This online textbook chapter is all about microbes.

http://serc.carleton.edu/microbelife/extreme/alkaline/index.html
Learn about microbes in alkaline lakes.

www.pbs.org/wgbh/nova/caves/extremophiles.html
Catch a *NOVA* interview with a biologist who is enthusiastic about studying extremophiles.

www.pbs.org/opb/intimatestrangers/index.html
This Public Broadcasting Service site has a lot to say about microbes, including archaeans.

www.theguardians.com/Microbiology/
The Guardians of the Millennium site for Microbiology includes resources on extremophiles and archaeans.

www.newscientist.com/
Articles and video clips from *New Scientist* magazine highlight some of the coolest new scientific discoveries. Do a search for "Archaea" or "extremophile."

Further Information–In Print

Breidahl, Harry. *Extremophiles: Life in Extreme Environments*. Chelsea House, 2002.

Index

Index

ABOUT THE AUTHORS

David M. Barker obtained his doctorate in zoology at The University of Texas at Austin. Since then, Dr. Barker has taught and worked as an editor and writer of science educational products in print and on the Web. In his spare time he enjoys practicing photography.